THE POPULATION OF DREAMS

poems by

Eugene Stevenson

Finishing Line Press
Georgetown, Kentucky

THE POPULATION OF DREAMS

Copyright © 2022 by Eugene Stevenson
ISBN 978-1-64662-736-3 First Edition
All rights reserved under International and Pan-American Copyright Conventions. No part of this book may be reproduced in any manner whatsoever without written permission from the publisher, except in the case of brief quotations embodied in critical articles and reviews.

ACKNOWLEDGMENTS

The author wishes to thank the editors of the following publications in which the poems first appeared:

Across the Pale White, *DASH Literary Review*
Against a Worry; Arc Light, *Icarus Quarterly*
Berryman, At the Bridge, *Chicago Tribune Magazine*
Bitters, *October Hill Magazine*
Dusty Springfield at Basin Street East, *Gravel Literary Review*
Loneliest Road in America, *The Poet Magazine*
Midnight Crossing the Picket Line, *Loch Raven Review*
Mosquito & Soul, *Angel City Review*
Overthink Tango, *South Florida Poetry Journal*
Plans to Leave, *Adelaide Literary Magazine*
Poncho Pays a Visit, *Gravel Literary Review*
The Population of Dreams, *Freshwater Literary Journal*
Union Station, Chicago, *Dime Show Literary Journal*
When the Call Came, *Swamp Ape Review*

Publisher: Leah Huete de Maines
Editor: Christen Kincaid
Cover Art: Eugene Stevenson
Author Photo: Lynn Ann Miller
Cover Design: Elizabeth Maines McCleavy

Order online: www.finishinglinepress.com
also available on amazon.com

Author inquiries and mail orders:
Finishing Line Press
PO Box 1626
Georgetown, Kentucky 40324
USA

Table of Contents

Midnight Crossing the Picket Line 1

Union Station, Chicago 3

Dusty Springfield at Basin Street East 5

Mosquito & Soul 7

Against a Worry 8

Banish the Owls 9

Across the Pale White 10

When the Call Came 11

Plans to Leave 13

Loneliest Road in America 15

For Viviana Matilde 24

Bitters 25

Arc Light 27

Berryman, At the Bridge 28

Poncho Pays a Visit 29

Overthink Tango 30

The Population of Dreams 32

For Gregory & Kathryn

Midnight Crossing the Picket Line

Pittsburgh. Midnight. The van driver has
no neck, wears sunglasses; his shaved head
grazes the headliner with each pothole,
each storm drain, each cross street, in a
winding route from an old & tired, third-rate
hotel to an old & tired, third-rate factory.

So little detail available through blacked-out
windows, the windshield becomes a movie
screen: frayed neighborhoods, wary clusters
engaged in street-corner commerce, the
odd bodega behind a scissor-grill & pull-down,
corrugated steel shutter, rusty & padlocked.

Mixed residential zoning cedes to industrial,
railroad tracks crisscross the streets, unfold
like a fan into a hundred sidings, where stone
from the quarries & chemicals mated from the
periodic table & wood from a million downed
trees trade places with a flow of finished goods.

Slow, gentle drift to the curb. Stop. Lights out.
Motionless. A soft voice from the driver's seat,
Keep quiet. Keep your eyes straight ahead.
Pull your collars up & your hats down. He has
not turned, stares straight ahead. *Keep quiet.*
Do not engage. Headlights. We round a corner.

Dim lights overhead. Lanterns & flashlights
turn in our direction. Shadows bent over
burn barrels straighten & turn to look at us.
The van moves slowly as do the dark figures on
the ground until they can thump the sides of
the vehicle & blister our birth & our mothers.

Placards swat the roof, kicks land on the tailgate
& back bumper. Then only the shouts. Then only
the hum of the tires on the asphalt leading to
a lighted, heavily guarded office. All over, with
less drama, less pain than anticipated. Crossing
the picket line is a gamble, a bet sometimes won.

Union Station, Chicago

1.

The ceiling is low, walls high,
lamps glare from all directions.
Light shafts like broom handles
poke the gut, stomach in throat.
Meals forgotten or uneaten. This
third day, which day of the week
unknown, ticket pocketed for
the six o'clock morning train, early,
the day will not be pea-green-lost.

2.

Cab driver quiet, transmission
smooth. Speed, centrifugal force
combine. Taxi wants to hurl its
passenger into the backward river,
but the ride continues, all the way to
the strange uncorner, to find a new
building there, new tunnels for
two-legged moles, naked, clothed,
running for the dark in the dark.

3.

The waitress is old, but age
has not dulled her sense of
humor. The sandwich is greasy &
good. Up high on the train board,
odd & even track numbers beckon
short- & long-distance travelers,
tear them from their phones.
Men walk like bullets.
Women walk like invitations.

4.

There are ghosts on the train:
lights go on & off like eyelids
out of kilter. Briefcase & bag are
companions, keep away old men,
talkative women, ill-smelling bodies.
Generators are the music, force
fantasies into the forehead's pain.
Pictures in the window pass &
time passes, most certainly, by.

5.

Not yet winter, but cold enough,
the wind batters, the lake is white
& angry. The faces in the crowd
are grim, wear their jaw-set masks
like shields, daring an engagement,
fearing an entanglement. On the
brick wall of a warehouse, a
painted ad proclaims *The House of
Time*. How long this minute lasts.

Dusty Springfield at Basin Street East

A black and white night even then,
her dress shimmers with black sequins in
the white stage lights, her diamond
earrings make an appearance as she swivels
that bouffant head of hers & the blonde hair
makes way like the Red Sea. Out it comes,
out of her captive lungs, that voice,
You don't have to say...
better than the recording. Her throat flexes
& moves, but she does not, fixed to
the small stage, a step or two away at most.

At the second table, the Filipinos,
four of them, offspring of politicians
& moguls, at ease in a night club,
the rich Irish girl from Nevada, eyes
wide, soft lips spread in a permanent
smile, & the Italian kid from New
York who still does not know how to
dress at 19, still does not know she
will leave him in a week for the
German ROTC stiff from Long Island,
& still does not know that a river
in its meandering will find the sea.

The plastic ashtray with its decal ID,
lifted, pocketed, as Buddy Rich flails
his hands & sticks in a hummingbird's
blur, the impossible grin, eyes looking
into the dark behind the lights, the
beat somewhere in his chest, carries
him & the crowd to a roar. But it is
Dusty who carries the place, the night,
into the decades ahead. The faces

recede, the property redeveloped, the
souvenir ditched in another move,
You don't have to say you love me.

Mosquito & Soul

Music flows out open doors
to night's dark stillness. In
the mosquito comes
flying circles, ovals, dashes until
its sharp needle finds the mark:
the sweet white flesh of
a soul exposed.

Three concerti:
the rise, the triumph, the fall.
Strings cease their vibrations,
yet chords echo against
streetlamps & thinning clouds.
Too late the door slides shut,
a spirit's sleep disturbed.

Against a Worry

Quiet disasters
two babies lost
one in snow
one in rain.

They were company
in their growing—
small swells
& promises.

I think of them
nestled in their
world of warmth
happy with discovery.

We hardly talk
but at night
thought comes hard
to pillowed heads.

Nourished briefly
in her suppleness
they have left her
open vulnerable.

She kneels frequently
her few prayers
earnest & strong
against a worry.

Banish the Owls

Slender ash to the east of the house,
standing in a row of trees, thin wall of
bark & green with late afternoon sun
providing a glaze of subdued yellow
with highlights of mellowed orange.

On a branch, aligned in one neat row,
four owls in silhouette, a well-executed
painting in oil or acrylic. One, closest to
the trunk, slightly larger, all immobile,
despite the chatter of child's play below.

The father first to notice, whispers to
the grandmother, then low-voiced calls
to the son & daughter. All gather, point
wide-eyed with whispers of wonder,
punctuated by successive *oohs & aahs*.

Grandmother disappears into the house,
emerges in a minute with the grandfather
who runs across the backyard, wild-eyed,
shouting *What are you trying to tell us?*
becoming suddenly an old-world fountain.

Across the Pale White

The woman, soft & grey
in her age, sits,
red hands extended
about a coffee cup,
her face the color of
the table top &
the snow outside.

Her words, spoken in
a whisper, but with
conviction, sketch her
family, her five children,
all grown, living away.
*I wouldn't do it again,
you know, the family I mean.*

With heavy finger through
the loop of the china,
she sips her coffee quietly,
without looking up,
without looking at her son,
seated across from her, across
the pale white of the table.

When the Call Came

When the call came in the middle of dinner
in Santiago, I walked off into the dark,
listened, looked into the night without
seeing a thing. *Last Rites* has a finality to it
even though some lucky bastards receive
it five or six times before they kick off.

In this case, my mother died the next morning,
just before my speech, delivered with the
punctuation, enthusiasm, crescendos, water
falls that mark my talks, but I could not hear
a single word of mine or theirs so don't know
what kind of answers I gave to the questions.

At dinner the night before, I was hungry, ate,
talked with colleagues, about what I don't know.
The table was outside on a stone patio, lights in
the dining room behind me, darkness in front.
I could not taste the color of the dishes, not
salty, not sweet, as if eating with my forehead.

Flights, Santiago-Miami, Miami-Somewhere,
Somewhere-Buffalo, more currents than clouds,
swept past cumulus on the bank, propelled on
thermals, not turbines. The rush of takeoff,
back pressed into the seat, floor canted
upward, missing, not there. No lift, no gravity.

By the time I arrived, forty-eight hours later, the
siblings had gathered, arrangements were set,
the funeral parlor had roses, roses without scent.
The Mass, the drive across the river, across the
border, so she could rest her rest with
her husband, her parents. So she could rest.

To this day, I cannot remember what she looked like in the casket, what the day was like when they lowered her into the ground. But I do see her face smile when she could no longer repeat her children's names in birth order, could not remember their names, so smiled.

Plans to Leave

In the early morning,
I make plans to leave.
Heavy clothes stay behind.
Boots & sandals, two suitcases
& a trench coat go.
Move in with a friend.
Find an undemanding job.
Rent a studio with a view,
settle in to read & write.
Ask for no entanglements.
Make no commitments.
Incur no debts.
Do the real work:
walk the streets, see all,
listen to the encountered.

By afternoon,
I have not moved from the desk.
Consider pain & responsibility.
Stare at the bookcase that
my hands built strong & ugly
for the love of books,
colored bindings, lives of
more solid men & women,
the bed behind me, waiting,
scene of more struggles than
months in my years. How
awkward, this, the heaviness of
the ex-piano player, the
one-time hockey player,
the former husband & lover.

That night,
the hot bed & damp sheets
seem crowded, thought
restless in its fear of being
read. Back turned, face to
the wall, the suitcases press
down with accusation, still
empty, still dusty on the shelf.
The passport remains in
its usual place while my
pillowed ear twitches with
each heartbeat, familiar sounds,
reminders that another day
has passed as I make plans
to leave, a move that cannot
take me from myself.

Loneliest Road in America

> *It is impossible to determine accurately both*
> *the position and the direction and speed of*
> *a particle at the same instant.*
>   —Werner Heisenberg

The loneliest road in America could be Route 50
across central Nevada, a road chosen from
the atlas two nights before, or could be the road
one chooses to drive solo, as an expert in leaving,
skills honed over years, over other roads,
the unsubtle ways of good-bye, so long.
In the car, everything? All one needs.

There are checkpoints to remind & guide:
a scratch on a rock, rocks, here & there
so I do not tread the same day twice. The charts
may need new markings after long sessions in
the treehouse. In the days before departure,
a repeated note to self: Do not expect,
do not expect at all, let alone too much.

1. Home

His father was a wandering soul. So he was
not, exchanged his trolley chits & railroad
passes for a three-lot plat where a brickyard
once stood, in a village upriver from an
orange-blue forest of open hearths &
chemical plants directly in the path of
prevailing winds that pushed translucent clouds
of chlorine & sodium ahead of coming storms.

He planted his feet in that plat, in that
village, planted the ash, the maples, the elms,
the lilacs, the honeysuckle, the poplars

to define his territory, with the bonus of
shade for the house, the yard, the garage.

There he grew, as much as his early life
would enable & allow, to witness his village
melded into the city, watch the ash tree in
front chainsawed to make way for a paved
road with granite curbs, oversee the removal
of the umbrellas, hubs, & tubes of diseased
backyard elms, show little regard as in
the space of an hour, saws ate the row of
poplars along the back lot line, their ambition
having outreached their strength. He watched
all that grew there in the yard & in the house,
watched it vanish, sooner than he knew
it would, much sooner than he expected.

Somewhere along the way, in his singular way,
he resolved to stay where he was until
his children were gone, his friends were gone,
his wife's mind was gone, his identity was gone.
Stay he did, until the night they carried him out
the front door of the house on a gurney, as if
practicing for the night, two weeks later, when
they carried him out of the rehab hospital
in a body bag & I walked him to the back door.

Before dawn, a too-bright light switched on,
I look at my father in the mirror, study his
specular reflection, squint until I decide the
better original light is this side of the silver glass,
behind the window glass, where he is wearing
clothes worn smooth under a grey wool jacket,
holes in the elastic cuffs, the jacket that gave
him his double-edged nickname. Now, in harsh

LED, he has a gift to give: the link between
going half crazy now & then, & when, after the
drama is over & pieces stop flying & settle down,
the dust also settles on all that has occurred.

2. East Ely

There are more Everests to die on than
we can count. Around Wheeler Peak,
13 thousand 63 feet, through Connors Pass,
77 hundred 22 feet, into this thin air
our last breath whispers as we ask,
if we can, *How did we get here?*
In East Ely, a whistle blows, a steam whistle.
The steam whistle blows again, unmistakably
a *Here I am*, an echo from the day
we lowered him into the ground.
Even when one flies for a living, for fun,
for fear, for need, even so there are stops.
I look for sense in the sound, for signals in
a coded message, for a face framed in
darkness with eyebrows like black nimbus,
eyes like sun through a magnifying glass,
lips like hell's rim speaking in brimstone.

Cigarette smoke out in the hallway drifts
down from the casino, all-machines & dark
as a barn. The Old Prospector has seen
better days, like the big-haired women of
a certain age, the big-hatted men of wizened
appearance, not entirely owing to age & sun.
This may not be a destination you choose,
but becomes a good enough place where
you decide to stay, counting your stacks of

dwindling chips, not counting how much
remains. In the *beep beep beep, boop boop*
of the money suckers, & the tinkling of ice
not yet melted by booze, a hollow comfort for
awhile, in that part of the day you throw away.

Early morning, Hotel Nevada coffee shop,
the waitress walks the counter, efficient,
omnipresent. *Another cup of coffee?*
Wanna top-up? She is catholic in preaching
her canon of abuse, *Ned's a regular, he doesn't*
getta please & thank you, doesn't get much
else neither. Breakfast theatre before sunrise.
Two coffees to go, the cups are small &
it's a stretch past hills of copper-mine tailings
to Eureka, a stretch where the feeling begins:
how far away all that is known, how far away
all that is recalled or remembered. Yet here
it is, all of it, populating the seat beside me,
populating satellite radio, populations
copulating in lyric & melody, as we climb
the east side, leaving the crowd behind,
behind Robinson Summit, 75 hundred 88 feet,
in a long slide to the valley floor, where
they gather once again in the back seat,
where they hitchhike along the shoulders in
both directions, where they recombine,
make faces & change faces, where they talk
to me or ignore me depending on what they
want. I am merely their chauffeur, heading
down the road west, west to what is there.

3. Eureka

All morning, all afternoon, all evening, all day,
everyday, *Welcome to Willie's Roadhouse,*
the home of Classic Country. We will never

have enough Willie Nelson, raw talent,
naiveté early, too-much-life late. This morning
he offers, *Nothing I Can Do About It Now*.
Flashbulbs blind, absent the *pop, pop, pop*.
Pull the car off gently on the west side of
the pass to take this photo: the road clings to
the mountainside in long arcs as it descends
to the right, north, then twists again & again,
finally to the left, west, across how many miles
until it rises to the right, north again, squeezes
into a gap in snow-headed peaks. Repeat in
forty minutes, repeat the sight, repeat, repeat.

I found it, The Owl Club cafe in Eureka, after
walking the elevated sidewalks on both sides
of the main drag, elevated for buckboards,
stage coaches, horses, Model-Ts. I am high,
having walked through an old postcard,
hand-painted to boast & to preen, not as
off-putting as the idea might seem, past the
general store with pizza among its offerings,
the court house, 1879 painted in black on
its white crown, the post office in a low shed.
Once, there was money & aspiration enough
to fill the red-brick opera house.

Gambling machines in the bar blare & glare
their one-measure melodies & cold, sharp lights.
Chicken-fried steak & hash browns, coffee as
good as it gets. Compliments to the chef, except
she is cheerless, looks puzzled before she says,
We get it from foodservice. A pause to note
we can be miserable or happy, maybe both
anywhere on the map or on the globe. Hitch
the jeans, walk in the sun & get out of town.

Over & through the mountains, miles & miles
of emptiness, better in a car with a good
engine & tires, wondrous at a Conestoga with
a pair of tired oxen & steel-rimmed wheels.
Up & over Hickison Summit 65 hundred 46 feet,
down to the valley floor, up & over Austin Summit
74 hundred 84 feet, cold headwind & country music
for company. Stomach full of breakfast, eyes full of
open road make for a good day, a celebration:
hall pass in the pocket, signed by Willie himself.

4. Cold Springs

Off Whiskey Hill, where the dead drink dust,
a pause to think of what might have been, but for
cotton flannel, virginity, a nightstand light &
a determined hand, meetings arranged in
subtraction of zip codes. This afternoon, the sun
is striated muscle, taut in the western sky.
To meet death on a blind curve, pass it by in
black & white, to see the kingdom of the missing
& the dead rise with each new ridge is to
make the u-turn a bigger part of the ride.
What a place to think, open space a luxury,
if you can spare the time from feeding stock,
scavenging wood for a fire, patching adobe walls.

Sage, scrub brush, tumbleweed wander by.
The stream that has etched a pass through
this topography is full with early April snow melt
heading east downhill to the Colorado.
The road mirrors the bank for miles, descends,
levels out, a safer place to mount the head
on a swivel, to see a carved & painted
wood sign, Pony Express Trail 1860-1861,
knowledge that deflates a boyhood myth.

At the ruins of the station, visions of bedding
down next to the animals for body heat,
falling asleep to wolves howling in the dark.
Here, a human history: Pony Bob rode
three hundred eighty miles roundtrip in
thirty-six hours after the local residents killed
a station manager, death by arrows if he was
lucky, retribution for the paleface incursion,
strong horses the prize worth killing for.

5. Carson City

The view out the windshield becomes jaded,
civilization is at hand to the right & left as
the highway broadens to four lanes, grows
traffic lights, fast food joints & strip malls
along its edges, & feeds duels with Buckeyes
tired from driving. Leave the road, divert north,
up through Silver City for a look at Virginia City,
quick read of bars & tourists, brief vision of
Hoss & the boys & their Canadian father,
back when characters had real conversations.
Drive by a large & unlikely Catholic church
looking more prosperous than the town
around it. Down to the pass, west again.

The route winds vaguely downhill, past signs
outside the city limits advertising local bordellos,
towards & through the state capital,
antiseptic like most state capitals.
Pedestrians more noteworthy: men in suits &
ties with briefcases, women in heels with
purses, & knots of tourists looking lost,
looking for lunch. Civilization makes one tired.

6. Tahoe

Diamonds sprawl on a blue silk runner, draw
the eyes, beyond tired in their sockets, to see
through a ragged, elongated green curtain.
Diamonds, more diamonds. More diamonds
than people, more diamonds than cars,
more diamonds than towns & stops on
the maps of the atlas. On the south shore of
the alpine lake where Nevada & California meet,
the driver, the wagon master, the traveler,
the wanderer, this generation's iteration of
the family genome untethered, looks though
the window of his room, looks north up the lake
& feels the water, the blood, the record of
the years, quiet down, the urge quelled, the itch
quelled, at least for the moment, a day or two.

There stretches from this place to the next,
a lonely road, asphalt with a single line, double
lines or no lines, muddy with rain, dusty with sun,
winding past ridge & mountain, past gulch &
valley, past sand & rock, past cliff face &
shattered stone, a path worn like a runner laid
across geography by these feet & the feet of
those who walked & rode before, those who
thought & spoke hopeful words a million times
before. Yet even in the residue of tumult, glacial
retreat, clash of tectonic plates, there are quiet
spaces of flowers watered by memories melting
like so many lemon drops on the tongue.

Save this history for another story, fit it in
between the dialogue, the faces, the names,
carry the record of the truths harvested from
this fragile soil. The highways into dreams are
darkened. Memory selects scenes illuminated
by dashboard light, high-wattage moonlight,
cloud-reflected city light, shaded sunlight,
all light & especially the light captured behind
the retina, filed or misfiled on the laptop, &
deep inside the repository of our history. No
Kerouac & Cassady on the road this time. This
is the flight again, multiplied, magnified, the
homestead far behind, but perennially in front
of the head. This solo drive over the loneliest
road in America has become less going-to than
leaving. No fooling the heart's odometer.

For Viviana Matilde

Yellow leaves atop green trees,
morning sun turns to aged alabaster,
brown cloud bleeds from the grey wet
canopy & muddies the creek below.

Water collects in curbside pools,
hard lines lost in small waved seas.
Perfect beauty: this strong soul in
a weakened body, lifted by the wind.

Music rises as a voice, muffled inside
fog, becomes a whisper. Blue behind
black, the mist in the sky's glass mirror
clears, the path ahead shows orange.

West light silhouettes a ridge, a promise,
Tomorrow, but at day's end, days end.
A grass berm, shorn flat, soaks in the rain,
soaks in moonlight. The lambs are asleep.

Bitters

What have you got on me,
to make this mattress
so unruly, unread
newspaper on the floor?
If at all the time was past,
the stone's throw picnic
of the hills & river stayed
until the black fright
storm died dry & fled.

Turned with words, basted,
wounds & all, with brine
to prickle the pink skin's
edges, the cuts rise to hold
printer's ink, high above a
textured page,
well beyond the rage of
childless women who
use those words to
different ends.

Listen to the song the
wind is turning on,
carry down the street.
Gull's wing clipped,
dog's nose dry,
sky bound with roses.
In translation
loses life & blood,
damned to isolation.
The skull, hard & sullen,
mocks the easy mash
of grey & ganglia.

Where I am is
where I have been
is where I have gone
is where I am going to be
in the middle of
the month: sea-horsed,
with lemon peel &
bitters inside me.

Arc Light

They are dying, the old men,
one by one.
the eyes close slowly
half-seeing still
what the world walks by.

Plugged into the sun, once,
the wires have frayed
from the insistent pulse
& now the energy,
expended for its worth,

filters through the recesses
of the sheets, of the walls
& folded maps of the world
read by arc light:
souls gathered for their flight.

Come awake, come awake.
The sky has cleared for hours.
Voices carried in the cold
make the travelers' work
less weary.

See the turn, there,
right around the corner?
Follow the white streaks
in their wind-wanderings.
Rest easy in sharp memory.

Berryman, At the Bridge

> *I broke a mirror, in which I figured you.*
> *—John Berryman*

Been there before: cold steel and water,
concrete support extension of the vertebrae,
cold will snap an angel's limb to calcium fluff.

A wave of the hand: greeting, dismissal, or resignation,
an act to signal the beginning and the end,
prelude and epilogue, the act is in the mind before it is.

And the leap: ah the heap to rejoin father and mistress,
the leap to the millennium, the continuum, and peace
like the river that never ends, alpha and omega.

Berryman, at the bridge, writes a poet's song,
and vaults the rail.

Poncho Pays a Visit

In the clinic, white, marbled, suffused,
staff wear no name badges, patients wear
no gowns. Difficult to ascertain who is who.
He is there, though, through the first place,
the second, into the third. Here it happens.

She sees him, sees that they notice him, in
all the places, one, two, and three. She says,
to no one in particular, *But he's dead, he's
dead.* Point to point to point, he is there on
a mission: clear up some unfinished business.

He is quiet as he turns, stands in the room
the way he always did, charms it, owns it,
inhales it, absorbs it, works the magic of
osmosis. He has shorn his beard as if it were
too much weight to carry after The Way.

Facing her, his eyes lock on to her eyes. The
voice, unexpected, *He's taking care of you.*
Up the switchback staircase to the right,
then the left, then through the solid wall,
he is gone, leaving a muffled sob behind.

Some time will need to pass, to settle this
account, before we learn if he has finished
with the vigil or pays another visit to deliver a
message or reminder or blessing. Question is
Will it be for the two of us or the three of us?

Overthink Tango

Follow the dancer after a tango
of their overthinking: nails out,
reopened flesh, red drips into
pools on the oriental carpet
older than their first meeting.
Drip, drip. Old Chinese torture.
They are their own torturers.

Fashionable to say *Let it go.*
Easy for others. December
thunder boomers bounce against
the ridges, rattle in the valleys to
the north, swell the creeks with
downpour so even rills slam angry
volume against their banks.

Temperatures will drop after this
rain, this storm, after the emails,
the texts, the phone calls slow.
One step at a time, one minute,
one day at a time until motion is
all there is, looking like curtains of
water sweeping the parking lot,

berms, streets, sidewalks, paths,
parks, stands of bending trees.
Gravity pulls the deluge into brown
streams, a hundred streams rush
downhill to seven rivers, through
watersheds into the bay, out to sea
from where their droplets rose.

Easy. Close the windows, muffle
the rumbles, wipe sill dry, drop
blinds, welcome darkness, brush
cheeks & find something to do,
trivial or otherwise, but keep close
counsel, forbid rain, evaporate flood.
Relegate today's tango to the bin.

The Population of Dreams

The number grows year by year,
the faces fresh as yesterday or today,
smiles as real as newly minted coins.

More often than not, they participate
in the storylines, no matter how
tortured or confusing or intricate.

My language deserts me this morning
as I try to reconcile my role long ago
in feeding whatever they had to accept.

Some nights, they play brief walk-ons,
others, speaking roles, in support of
the lead. After all, the script is mine.

Entrance right: they walk into the room,
eye contact, a pause in the step, smiles
either flood or pinpoint the scene in light.

Center stage, back of the head, curls so
familiar, I could extend my hand to touch,
but do not, wait for her to turn, face me.

Stage left, head down, turns to throw me
the stink-eye, disapprobation even I
could not miss or mistake for greeting.

Or worse, somewhere in the second act,
music fades, sounds of activity here rise,
upturned lips turn down. Cold surrounds.

The day is littered with thoughts of night,
the daily rushes flicker back to who they
were, the population of those dreams.

Eugene Stevenson is the son of immigrants, the father of expatriates. He writes to make some semblance of order out of disorder, to make sense of the unthinkable, to make still photographs out of daily rushes. His poems have appeared in numerous literary journals. His prose has appeared in *The New York Times* & *Los Angeles Times*. He is an American Field Service Scholar & an Eisenhower Fellow. He lives in the mountains of western North Carolina.

www.ingramcontent.com/pod-product-compliance
Lightning Source LLC
LaVergne TN
LVHW041347080426
835512LV00006B/653